MAKE YOUR OWN
THERMAL
OVEN

THE SELF-RELIANT METHOD FOR FASTER, FLUFFIER BREAD

Caleb Warnock

 THE BACKYARD RENAISSANCE COLLECTION

DISCOVER THE LONG-LOST SKILLS OF SELF-RELIANCE

y name is Caleb Warnock, and I've been working for years to learn how to return to forgotten skills, the skills of our ancestors. As our world becomes increasingly unstable, self-reliance becomes invaluable. Throughout this series, *The Backyard Renaissance*, I will share with you the lost skills of self-sufficiency and healthy living. Come with me and other do-it-yourself experimenters, and rediscover the joys and success of simple self-reliance.

FAMILIUS

Published by Familius LLC, www.familius.com

Familius books are available at special discounts for bulk purchases for sales promotions or for family or corporate use. Special editions, including personalized covers, excerpts of existing books, or books with corporate logos, can be created in large quantities for special needs. For more information, contact Premium Sales at 559-876-2170 or email specialmarkets@familius.com.

Library of Congress Catalog-in-Publication Data
2015942862   ISBN 9781942672951

Edited by Liza Hagerman
Cover design by David Miles
Book design by David Miles and Brooke Jorden

10 9 8 7 6 5 4 3 2 1
First Edition

CONTENTS

INTRODUCTION

D id you know that a thermal oven, which utilizes neither electricity nor gas, can raise up to ten loaves of bread dough, or forty-eight cinnamon rolls or dinner rolls? You can also use it to make homemade yogurt, cook thousands of recipes for lunch or dinner, or chill or freeze foods at home and on the go. Its versatility makes it useful every day, in emergencies, for preparation, or for traveling. A thermal oven may be purchased, but later I will show you how to make your own!

Using a thermal oven is the cheapest, fastest, easiest, and most reliable way to raise bread dough made from natural yeast. Thermal ovens were used to raise bread dough for centuries! In fact, the word "oven" is a misnomer, because thermal ovens also act as freezers and coolers, as we will discuss later.

The basic concept of a thermal oven, whether you are cooking or chilling food, or raising bread dough, is to trap heat. Centuries ago, thermal cooking was accomplished by heating a pan over a fire and then wrapping the pan overnight in a feather or straw mattress. The mattress retained the heat, allowing the food to cook away from the fire once the pan was heated.

There are endless ways to design a modern thermal cooker, but in this book I will introduce you to my Two-in-One Thermal Oven—the only design that allows you to inexpensively create a homemade thermal oven that will proof, or raise, up to eight loaves of bread at once, or two trays of cinnamon rolls or dinner rolls!

My design was born of necessity. Today, there is a free pattern available online that shows people how to make a fabric thermal oven. I have one of these, which I purchased from a friend's daughter for fifty dollars. The simple fabric oven has four seams and holds a cooking pot or a bread pan. However, I found a problem with the design. I love to make homemade natural yeast cinnamon rolls, and there is no way to raise such rolls in a traditional thermal oven because the oven is too small to fit anything larger than a single bread pan—there is no room for a sheet of rolls. Additionally, I needed an oven that could raise several loaves of bread at once. I sometimes need to make eight loaves at a time, because I teach large classes and conferences based on my book, *The Art of Baking with Natural Yeast*, which I coauthored with natural yeast expert Melissa Richardson. I wanted to be able to take warm bread, fresh out of the oven, to my classes, and I wanted to use a thermal oven to proof my dough for cinnamon and dinner rolls, too. I searched for a thermal oven that would allow me to make anywhere from one to eight loaves of bread, or homemade yogurt, or two trays of cinnamon rolls (forty-eight rolls total).

There was no such thermal oven.

So I created my own. As I write this book, it only costs about twenty dollars to make an oven of my design. You can even make one for free—I will explain how in a later chapter.

WHAT EXACTLY IS A THERMAL OVEN?

A thermal oven is any kind of insulated container that can be used to cook food, chill food, or raise bread. Historically, these were often wooden boxes lined with straw, wood shavings, or, best of all, wool. The heat for cooking comes in one of two ways—either the cooking pan is heated for a few minutes before being put into the thermal oven, or a hot stone, heated water, or coals are put into a container and placed on the bottom of the thermal cooker, and the food is then placed on top, in its own container.

A thermal oven typically has two parts—the container and the lid. The container can be a box or something purpose-built that looks like a pillow in a bowl shape. The lid, which is essentially a pillow, is used to cover it.

When you are raising bread dough, nothing else works quite as well as a thermal oven. The consistent, prolonged warmth helps the bread become more spongy and fluffy than with any other method I have been able to find. No wonder people have used thermal ovens to raise bread for centuries!

The first-ever commercial thermal oven appears to have been the Norwegian Self-Acting Cooker, which was patented in 1869. Before then, thermal ovens were homemade. Thermal oven cookers are also sometimes called fireless cookers, straw box cookers, hay boxes, wonder boxes, insulation cookers, heat-retained cookers, etc. Historically, any number of natural materials has been used for insulation, including:

- Hay
- Straw

- Wood shavings
- Sawdust
- Wool
- Dried moss
- Cotton or used fabric
  Modern materials include:
- Styrofoam beads
- Foam board
- Shredded paper
- Polyester batting

HOW TO CONTAIN YOUR PROOFING DOUGH

N o matter what kind of dough you are making, it will rise best in a thermal oven.

When using a thermal oven to raise bread, you need to cover your dough, and there are several ways to do this.

COVERED BREAD PANS

T here is one big difference between the way people raised bread dough historically and the way most people do it today. Most commercial bakeries have caught on and gone back to the "ancient method"—using covered pans.

Today, bread pans are often sold without lids, but in the past, bread pans always had lids. I have a collection of antique glass bread pans, each with a glass lid. You can find these for sale on eBay or in antique stores—I have purchased them from both sources. Some are plain and some are more decorative, but these old-fashioned bread pans are no longer manufactured because few people use natural yeast anymore. (Melissa and I explain the health benefits of natural yeast versus commercial yeast in our book, *The Art of Baking with Natural Yeast*, which is available on Amazon and at other online and brick-and-mortar retailers.)

CUTTING BOARDS

hen I am making loaves of bread, I use antique covered loaf pans both for proofing and baking. (I bake my bread, rolls, etc in a traditional oven, because bread baked in a thermal oven does not brown). But when I am making dinner rolls or cinnamon rolls—my favorite—I put the raw rolls into 9- by 13-inch glass casserole dishes (greased, of course) and cover them with plastic or wood cutting boards. I then put these dishes inside the thermal oven on top of the heat source (hot water—more on this in a moment) and cover them with the thermal oven lid, or blankets. This gives the rolls space to rise without the dough getting the fabric oven dirty or the lid of the oven pressing down on the dough. Make sure your pan is deep enough that the rolls don't touch the top.

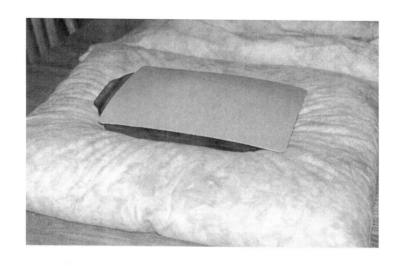

HOW TO HEAT A THERMAL OVEN FOR PROOFING DOUGH

ny hot object will work as a heat source for your thermal oven, but I prefer hot water. If I am raising one or two loaves, I put the hottest tap water I can get into a rubber hot water bottle (available

at any pharmacy). I fill the bottle three-quarters full, press out any air inside, close it, and place it in the bottom of the thermal oven. I put the covered bread pans on top of the bottle and then cover the whole thing with the lid to the thermal oven.

If I am raising more than two loaves of bread, or if I am making cinnamon rolls or dinner rolls, I put the hottest tap water I can get into a resealable plastic bag, close the bag, and then put it inside a second resealable plastic bag as a precaution against leaking. I place one or two of these bags under each dish holding the rolls or bread dough. Then I cover the thermal oven with the lid.

You could also use water heated on the stove if you put it in a container that will not melt, and if you can safely handle the water. I don't recommend using boiling water because of the danger of burns.

PREVENTING HEAT LOSS

Thermal ovens work best when there is as little air space inside them as possible. If you have empty air space around your bread pans, put dishcloths, towels, or fabric scraps in these "dead" spaces. Dead air space draws heat away from your bread pan and allows the heat to move around inside the thermal oven. You retain heat best when there are as few air spaces as possible.

Make sure the thermal oven is sealed tightly. Whether you are using a blanket oven, a homemade fabric oven, a homemade box oven, or an expensive, store-bought thermal oven, the oven lid needs to cover the container completely and have no air gaps. When using a fabric or blanket oven, press the fabric lid all the way around the top of the oven to make sure there are no small folds or creases that will allow the heat to escape. A tight lid means your oven is well insulated and hot. A loose lid means your oven will quickly lose heat.

HOW TO MAKE A THERMAL OVEN FOR FREE

ny blanket can be used to make a thermal oven if you follow a couple of simple suggestions, but historically, wool blankets have been deemed to work the best, because wool has a higher R-value than cotton or straw.

R-value is the term that scientists use to describe the thermal resistance of a material. Thermal resistance refers to the ability of a material to trap heat. If you live in a cold climate, you have insulation in your walls to help trap the heat from your furnace inside your home. A good insulation barrier makes heat escape much more slowly than it would if your walls had no insulation. In this respect, a thermal oven is just like your home, only on a much smaller scale. Your home has a lid (the roof), four walls, and a bottom, just like a thermal oven. A thermal oven encloses a cooking pot with insulation so that the heat escapes as slowly as possible. Trapping the heat makes it possible to cook food, keep food warm, keep cold food chilled, or keep frozen food frozen for hours. You can find the R-values of many different materials, including straw, cotton, and sheep's wool, by visiting the "Insulation Materials" page at Energy.gov.

Here are instructions for building a homemade thermal oven for free:

1. Use three blankets if possible. Fold a blanket in half if you want and, for convenience, lay it out on a large flat surface, such as a bed or table. Fold the second blanket in half and lay it on top of the first blanket; repeat with the third blanket. The blankets, whether folded or not, should cover the entire pan, leaving no open spaces.

2. Before putting anything inside your blanket "oven," move the blankets to a flat place where you can leave them undisturbed for many hours, and possibly overnight.

3. First, place your heat source (such as a hot water bottle) in the center of the flat blankets. Next, place

your bread pan or container directly over the heat source. Put the lid tightly on the pan or container. Then, fold the flat blankets over the container, so that the dough and container are in the center of the blanket oven. Press down the blankets all the way around the dough container to make sure there are no small folds or creases that will allow the heat to escape.

Leave the thermal oven undisturbed for several hours. If you are using commercial rapid-rise or quick-rise yeast, your dough may rise after 2–3 hours. If you are using natural yeast, you can check it after four hours or leave it as long as overnight. If you open the oven for more than a moment, you will need to replace the hot water.

If you are using natural yeast, replace the hot water once in a ten- to twelve-hour cycle. To replace the hot water, simply open the thermal oven, take out the water and food containers, empty and refill the hot water container with the hottest tap water you can get, replace the water container, put the food container on top of it, and close the lid to the thermal oven.

6 When the dough has doubled in size, you can either bake your bread or rolls, or punch them down in the traditional manner and let them rise a second time before baking. Bake according to your recipe instructions. For natural yeast baking recipes, refer to my book, *The Art of Baking with Natural Yeast*, co-authored by Melissa Richardson.

IF YOU NEED A FREE NATURAL YEAST START, VISIT CALEBWARNOCK.BLOGSPOT.COM AND CLICK ON "FREE OFFERS" NEAR THE TOP OF THE PAGE.

CALEB'S TWO-IN-ONE THERMAL OVEN

ou will need:

- 2 pieces of fabric, each 1 yard by 2 yards
- Shredded paper, fabric scraps, or polystyrene beads for filler.

For a link to the best price for polystyrene beads, visit: www.calebwarnock.blogspot.com/2014/09/making-homemade-thermal-oven.html

1. Enclose each piece of fabric to become a pillow. This means you will have two pillows when you are finished. This can be done by machine stitching or hand stitching, or with fusible fabric bonding tape (e.g., Stitch Witchery, which is ironed on and does not require sewing). The type of fabric you use is up to you—any kind will work. When I made my original thermal oven, I used fusible bonding tape, but after several months of use, the bonding tap began to loosen and I used a needle and thread to permanently sew the pillows together. This took only a few minutes.

2. Turning the fabric inside out, fuse or sew the fabric to form a square pillow. Leave an opening of a few inches so that the filler can be inserted into the pillow.

3. Fill each of the two pillows with your filler, which can be shredded paper, fabric scraps, or polystyrene

beads. If you are using the beads, pour slowly—spilled polystyrene beads are no fun to clean up! I suggest cutting a small hole in the corner of your bag of beads, putting this hole directly into the opening in your homemade container, and pouring slowly with the help of a second person. You *do not* want to fill the pillows so full that they are stiff. Start by filling them three-quarters full, and then testing them by pinning the fabric opening closed temporarily while you try using your thermal oven. Remember that there needs to be enough "give" or room in each pillow for bread pans or cooking containers to nestle inside.

Using fusible tape or stitching, close up the opening you used to fill the pillow. Next, repeat this process with your second piece of fabric, creating a second pillow. One pillow will be your thermal oven, and the second pillow will be the "lid." Your thermal oven is now ready to use.

PROOFING LARGE BATCHES

se the thermal oven pillows in a flat position for large batches of bread, or for dinner rolls or cinnamon rolls. Put the container on a flat surface where it can be left undisturbed for several hours (I use the kitchen table or the desk in my home office). Put the heat source, such as a hot water bottle, into the center. Put the rolls or bread, in their covered pans, directly over the heat source, then put the lid on top.

PROOFING ONE OR TWO LOAVES, OR COOKING IN A POT

or a cooking pot, or for one or two loaves of bread, follow these steps:

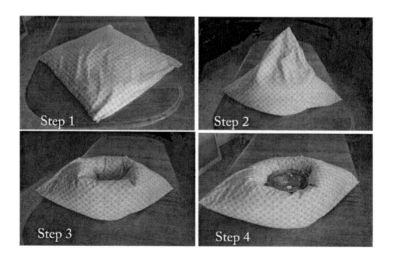

1 Lay the bottom pillow (the container) on a flat surface so it forms a diamond shape.

2 Pick up the pillow by the top corner and hold it above your flat surface.

3 Lower it down onto the bottom corner of the diamond, allowing it to collapse into a pile. Adjust the pillow to create a space in the center.

4 Place your heat source, such as a hot water bottle, into the center of the container. Next, place a bread pan or cooking pan directly over the heat source.

5 Cover with the "lid"—the top pillow.

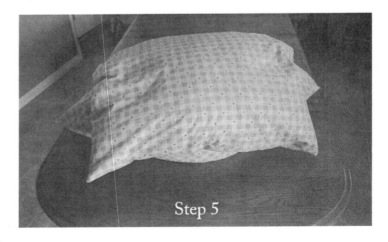

Step 5

PROOFING IN BAGS

I have also used plastic food bags (available at your local grocery store) to raise dough in a thermal oven. The advantage of using a bag is that the dough remains moist and the top does not dry out. Many bakeries and pizza restaurants raise their dough in greased bags or lidded plastic containers.

First, I grease the bag by putting one and a half teaspoons of olive oil or liquid coconut oil into the bag. I press the outside of the bag to move the oil around to coat the entire inside of the bag. I put the kneaded dough into the bag and then close the bag carefully with a twist tie so that I have enough air space trapped in the bag for the dough to double in size. I then put the whole bag into the thermal oven, on top of my hot water container. When the dough has proofed, I can use it for scones or put it directly into a greased and floured bread pan to bake in the oven.

USING YOUR OVEN AS A CHILLER OR TRAVEL FREEZER

Thermal ovens can also be used to retain cold temperatures for hours. Simply put chilled or frozen containers of food into the thermal oven and cover with the lid. Remember, for best results, use dishcloths or towels to fill any empty space around your chilled or frozen container inside the thermal oven. This is great for taking ice cream when driving to a party or picnic, etc. Or you can use a thermal oven to keep food chilled when your refrigerator is full, if you are hosting Thanksgiving dinner at your home, or when you are traveling to a dinner party or family gathering, for instance.

FOOD SAFETY AND RECOMMENDED READING

F ood that is cooked or chilled in a thermal oven must be maintained at safe temperatures. Please read the US Department of Health and Human Services' "Integrated Food Safety Information Delivery System (IFSIDS)" fact sheet. However, remember that these guidelines do not apply to raising dough in a thermal oven, because the dough will be cooked at full temperature later. The guidelines only apply to actually cooking and keeping food cool in a thermal oven. To find and read the guidelines, please visit www.profoodsafety.org.

For historic thermal oven recipes and instructions, read:

- *The Fireless Cook Book* by Margaret J. Mitchell (published 1909). www.archive.org/details/firelesscookbook00mitc
- *The Fireless Cooker: How To Make It, How To Use It, What To Cook* by Caroline Barnes Lovewell, Frances Dean Whittemore, and Hannah Wright Lyon (© 1908). bit.ly/1wK8LgC

- "Rediscover Haybox Cooking" by Bonnie M. Arnold www.motherearthnews.com/diy/haybox-cooking-zmaz80jfzraw.aspx#axzz3EA98ts00

BONUS: CREATING A NATURAL YEAST START

Creating a yeast start from nature for baking could not be easier. Natural yeast makes wheat flour gluten free. The yeasts eat the gluten. Grocery store yeast, which has been modified, does not make flour gluten free because the modified yeast does not eat the gluten. Modified yeast is quick or rapid rising. Natural yeast has not been sold in stores for many years. Natural yeast also flattens the glycemic index, prevents heartburn and acid reflux when used with whole wheat, and is both prebiotic and probiotic. To "create" a natural yeast start from nature, all you need is wheat.

There are more than a thousand species of the yeast fungi known to science. Some of them are great for making bread, some for making wine, and others for making beer. Natural yeast is not completely a dead art—some bakeries in Europe and even North America continue to capture natural yeast from the wild to make their breads. Where do they get their starts? From wheat. Yeast is everywhere in nature—in the air and on the leaves of plants and trees. Yeasts appear to be naturally drawn to the food source that suits them best—the yeast species that are best for making bread congregate on wheat, while other species congregate on grapes or hops, for example.

I grow wheat in my backyard, but you can use any freshly harvested wheat to make a yeast start. Be sure the wheat you are using is organic and has not been sprayed with any chemicals. If needed, you can purchase organic Turkey Red Winter wheat kernels from my garden at SeedRenaissance.com. Here's how to get "started":

1. Put one head of freshly harvested wheat, or one teaspoon of freshly harvested wheat kernels, into a glass mason jar. Add 1 cup of lukewarm purified water. Do not use chlorinated water. Add 1 heaping cup of flour (I use whole wheat flour). Mix these together in the jar.

2. Set the jar on your kitchen counter out of direct sunlight for 24–48 hours. During this time, the mixture in your jar will become bubbly yeast. When it increases in size in the jar, sieve out the wheat heads or wheat kernels by pouring the yeast mixture through a sieve into a bowl. Throw out the kernels or heads of wheat.

3. You now have a live natural yeast start to be used for baking. Your natural yeast is a living organism.

4. It will be hungry. Feed it as immediately as possible. Here is the "recipe" for feeding it:

- 1 part live natural yeast (already contained in your jar)
- 1 part purified water
- 1 heaping part flour (I recommend whole wheat, but any flour—even gluten-free—works).

- The "part" can be any measurement. One-half cup is a good "part" to start with.

Your yeast is ready to use for cooking or baking when it is filled with bubbles. The bubbles can be any size, but they must be all throughout the yeast. If you want to move your yeast to the refrigerator to slow its growth, remove most of the yeast (you can use it to cook, use it in a green smoothie, or throw it out), feed what is left in the jar by stirring in flour and water, and put it in the refrigerator. Feed it twice a week in the refrigerator. Before you cook or bake with the refrigerated yeast, remove it from the refrigerator, divide it, feed it, and let it sit on the counter until it is filled with bubbles of any size. It does not necessarily need to double in size.

If you are new to using natural yeast, the process of baking with real yeast is not at all like using yeast from the grocery store. For recipes, instructions, and health benefits, see *The Art of Baking with Natural Yeast*, coauthored by Melissa Richardson and me.

TIPS

our family for generations before you used natural yeast for all of their baking, even your family members who had no access to education. They did it, and you can, too!

- *Never* use tap water. Water with chlorine damages the natural yeast, which is a living fungus. Purified water is better than distilled water, better than tap water, and better than spring water. Most of the problems that people encounter with natural yeast seem to stem from either feeding the yeast too infrequently or using chlorinated water. Some people are able to successfully use tap water, but be wary because the chlorine levels in treated water change constantly—they change by the season, by region, and even by the hour depending on testing done by water managers. So while your chlorinated water may seem to work fine one day—or even for months—your yeast may suddenly begin to seem sluggish and sick because the chlorine levels in your tap water have increased. For this reason,

I strongly recommend never using tap water for natural yeast. Remember that natural yeast is an ancient technology and has been used for thousands of years, but in all of history, modern generations are the first that have had to adjust for chlorinated water.

- Baking bread, rolls, and cinnamon rolls is the *hardest* thing you can do with natural yeast because they require precision when kneading and proofing. They are an art and will take time and patience to perfect. In the meantime, do what is easy—muffins, pancakes, waffles, and scones. The goal is to get the natural yeast into your body so it can help restore your health. You can do this for the rest of your life without ever making bread. Make health your goal by doing what is easy first! You can also mix raw natural yeast into your green smoothies.

- As a general rule, natural yeast is 95 percent gluten-free after rising for twenty-four hours, 97 percent gluten-free after thirty-six hours, and 98 percent gluten-free after forty-eight hours. You don't have to take my word for it— you can test this yourself by purchasing a home gluten test kit (each costs several hundred dollars).

- Most people with wheat allergies or gluten intolerance see their allergy or intolerance vanish after eating natural yeast two to three times a week for a month, though results may vary. Most people are eventually able to add store-bought and restaurant breads back into their diet slowly as long as they continue to use natural yeast two to three times a week.

ABOUT THE AUTHOR

aleb Warnock is the popular author of *Forgotten Skills of Self-Sufficiency Used by the Mormon Pioneers*, *The Art of Baking with Natural Yeast*, *Backyard Winter Gardening For All Climates*, *More Forgotten Skills*, *Trouble's On The Menu*, and the Backyard Renaissance Collection. He is the owner of SeedRenaissance.com and blogs at CalebWarnock.blogspot.com, where you will find a link to join his email list to learn more about forgotten skills.

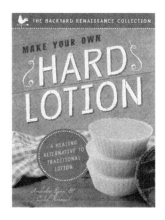

ABOUT FAMILIUS

VISIT OUR WEBSITE: www.familius.com

JOIN OUR FAMILY: There are lots of ways to connect with us! Subscribe to our newsletters at www.familius.com to receive uplifting daily inspiration, essays from our Pater Familius, a free ebook every month, and the first word on special discounts and Familius news.

GET BULK DISCOUNTS: If you feel a few friends and family might benefit from what you've read, let us know and we'll be happy to provide you with quantity discounts. Simply email us at specialorders@familius.com.

CONNECT:

www.facebook.com/paterfamilius
@familiustalk, @paterfamilius1
www.pinterest.com/familius

FAMILIUS

THE MOST IMPORTANT WORK YOU EVER DO WILL BE WITHIN THE WALLS OF YOUR OWN HOME.

CPSIA information can be obtained at www.ICGtesting.com
Printed in the USA
BVOW02s2019020316

438848BV00001B/3/P